D0408320

Isaiah's MESSIAH

VICTOR BUKSBAZEN, TH.D.

THE FRIENDS OF ISRAEL GOSPEL MINISTRY, INC.

Isaiah's MESSIAH
Victor Buksbazen, Th.D.
Copyright © 2002 by The Friends of Israel Gospel Ministry, Inc.
P.O. Box 908, Bellmawr, NJ 08099
Excerpted and revised from *The Prophet Isaiah* by Victor Buksbazen.
Original Copyright © 1971 by The Spearhead Press.
Library of Congress Catalog Card Number 76-178967

Fourth Printing 2014

Library of Congress Catalog Card Number   2002101925
ISBN-10 0-915540-75-4
ISBN-13 978-0-915540-75-4

Drawings by Stan Stein.
Cover and layout by Lori Winkelman.

Translation of Isaiah from Hebrew to English by Dr. Victor Buksbazen.
All Scripture other than Isaiah is quoted from *The New Scofield Study Bible,*
Authorized King James Version, Oxford University Press, Inc., 1967.

Visit our website at www.foi.org.

TABLE OF CONTENTS

FOREWORD

For thirty-three years Dr. Victor Buksbazen served with extreme distinction as the executive director of the organization that would mature into The Friends of Israel Gospel Ministry. The Buksbazens, Victor and Lydia, were exemplary embodiments of the culture, refinement, grace, and gentility of pre–World War II Europe. Following his education at the University of Warsaw, Victor served as a reserve officer in the Polish army. After escaping the horrors of Hitler's Europe, the Buksbazens settled in England where they endured the rigors of the dark days of the blitz.

Upon coming to America, Victor was appointed executive director of the fledgling Friends of Israel Missionary and Relief Society. The founders of the organization could not have made a better choice. Dr. Buksbazen spoke nine languages fluently and was a true scholar in the area of biblical studies and rabbinic Judaism. His mastery of languages and understanding of rabbinic interpretation made him a rare and effective individual in the Christian world. In the view of many, including myself, Victor ranks in scholarship and quality with the revered Dr. Alfred Edersheim. This unique volume treats you to Victor's erudite translation of Isaiah 52—53.

In describing Victor's superb qualities, one writer once commented, "He possesses the simplicity of the child, the faith of a great soul, the knowledge of a scholar, and the courage of a great missionary, a heart afire for service. His instincts are sweet and virtuous, his mind lofty, ardent and quick with the irresistible fire of an apostle."

As you read the pages that follow, you will gain a refreshing glimpse into the mind and soul of a man we know too little of—one who established the bedrock of integrity and direction of the ministry of The Friends of Israel. Beyond all this, however, you will receive a scholarly, thoroughly scriptural, and decidedly Jewish look into the message of the suffering Messiah of Isaiah 53 through the eyes of one who, as a Jew, had himself been through the crucible of affliction and found rest at the foot of the cross.

Elwood McQuaid

I.

THE CONTROVERSY

The prophecy of Isaiah 52:13—53:12 is the heart of the second section of the book of Isaiah, called the Book of Consolation. Here Messianic vision reaches its pinnacle. For almost two millennia, Jewish and Christian scholars have debated the question of whether the prophet was speaking of himself or of Israel who suffers innocently for the nations of the world. In the New Testament, the Ethiopian eunuch who was reading Isaiah 53 touched on the heart of this question when he asked Philip, the early disciple of

Christ, "I pray thee, of whom speaketh the prophet this? Of himself, or of some other man?" (Acts 8:34).

ORIGINAL RABBINICAL VIEW: THE SERVANT IS MESSIAH

Generally, there is little difference between Jewish and Christian translations of this majestic passage of Isaiah, apart from a few words of secondary importance. However, there is a profound and basic difference in the interpretation of the text. For many centuries, ancient Jewish tradition has seen Isaiah 53 as a portrait of God's suffering servant, the Messiah—a view that is held to this day by most Orthodox Jews.

However, at the end of the 11th century A.D., a change took place. Jewish commentators began to assert that Isaiah spoke of Israel, who suffers innocently for the sins of all nations.

Christians, following the ancient Jewish tradition, maintain that Isaiah 53 speaks of Messiah. Consequently, they see it as an amazing prophecy concerning Jesus, "the Lamb of God, who taketh away the sin of the world" (Jn. 1:29).

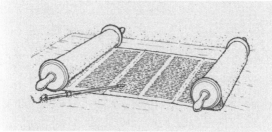

Which interpretation is correct? Only one coincides with the meaning of the words and the context of Isaiah's message, preached more than 700 years before Jesus' birth. And only one interpretation contains the true message that God wants to convey to His beloved people, Israel. We shall examine the controversy: Is Jehovah's suffering servant Israel, or is he Jesus?

Going back to the oldest Jewish interpretations of this passage, we find that the Targum of Jonathan ben Uziel (2nd century A.D.), an Aramaic paraphrase of the Bible, renders Isaiah 52:13 in this way:

Behold my servant Messiah shall prosper; he shall be high, and increase and be exceedingly strong.

The Babylonian Talmud (codified in the 6th century) also applies Isaiah's prophecy messianically:

*The Messiah—what is his name? . . . The Rabbis say,
"the leprous one:" Those of the house of Rabbi say,
"the sick one," as it is said, "surely he hath borne our
sickness" (San 98b).*

Midrash Rabbah, referring to Ruth 2:14, explains,

*He is speaking of the King Messiah: "Come hither
draw near to the Throne; and eat the bread," that is
the bread of the kingdom: "and dip thy morsel in the
vinegar." This refers to his chastisements, as it is said,
"But he was wounded for our transgressions, bruised
for our iniquities."*

In the Yalkut Shimoni, a later *Midrash* (rabbinical
commentary), it is written,

*"Who art thou, O great mountain?" (Zech. 4:7).
This refers to the King Messiah, And why does he call
him "the great mountain?" Because He is greater
than the patriarchs. As it is said, "My servant shall
be high and lifted up and lofty exceedingly." He will
be higher than Abraham, who says, "I raise high my
hand unto the Lord" (Gen. 14:22). Lifted up above
Moses, to whom it is said, "Lift it up into thy bosom"*

(Num. 11:12): Loftier than the ministering angels, of whom it is written: "Their wheels were lofty and terrible" (Ezek. 1:18).

These are only a few of the many rabbinical comments

WHAT CAUSED SUCH A RADICAL CHANGE IN THE RABBINICAL POSITION?

relating to Isaiah 52:13—53:12 that, with one accord, apply the section to the Messiah. What caused such a radical change in the rabbinical position?

CURRENT RABBINICAL VIEW: THE SERVANT IS ISRAEL

Behind this change lies the tragic Jewish experience during the Crusades. After the end of the First Crusade in A.D. 1096, when the Crusaders, in their misguided zeal, attempted to wrest the Holy Sepulcher from the Muslims, they became aware that the infidels were not only "the pagan Muslims" in faraway Palestine but also "the Christ-killing Jews" who were living in their very midst, in so-called Christian Europe. Encouraged by their fanatical leaders and frequently incited by high-ranking clerics, the Crusaders began massacring Jewish people, especially those who lived in France, Italy, and Germany. Thousands were butchered, their synagogues burned, and their possessions pillaged.

This horrible experience, which lasted for almost two centuries, left a traumatic impact on the Jewish people comparable only to their later experience under Adolph Hitler. From that time on, their revulsion against everything Christians believed or represented became more violent and hostile than ever.

And since the Christians, in their frequent disputes with the Jewish people, used Isaiah 53 as one of their main arguments for the messiahship of Jesus, Jewish people felt impelled to reinterpret this prophecy in such a way as to blunt the Christian argument. Since then, the question of Isaiah 53 has taken on a heated polemical and emotional character.

Another compelling reason to abandon the Messianic interpretation of the controversial passage was that many Jewish people themselves became convinced that a cogent and strong argument exists for the Christian position. In fact, many actually embraced the Christian faith as a result of the Christian-Jewish disputations of the Middle Ages. During that period, the outstanding Jewish scholar R. Joseph Ben Kaspi (1280–1340) warned the rabbis that "those who expounded this section of the Messiah give occasion to the heretics [Christians] to interpret it of Jesus." About this statement Rabbi Saadia ibn Danan observed, "May God forgive him for not having spoken the truth."[1]

In any case, since A.D. 1096, Jewish interpreters began to teach that Isaiah's suffering servant was not the Messiah but, rather, persecuted and suffering Israel, "who is brought as a lamb to the slaughter, and as a sheep . . . openeth not his mouth" (Isa. 53:7).

In light of the Crusaders' atrocities, this interpretation took on a semblance of verisimility and found much favor among the majority of Jews—but not among all of them. Still the original Messianic interpretation of Isaiah 53 persisted and survives even to the present day.

THE CONTROVERSY

It is preserved in Jewish liturgy for the Day of Atonement (*Yom Kippur*) in a prayer attributed to Eliezer Ha-Kallir (8th century A.D.):

> *We are shrunk up in our misery even until now! our rock hath not come nigh to us: Messiah, our righteousness, hath turned from us; we are in terror, and there is none to justify us! Our iniquities and the yoke of our transgressions he will bear,* **for he was wounded for our transgressions:** *he will carry our sins upon his shoulder, that we may find forgiveness for our iniquities, and* **by his stripes we are healed.** *O eternal One, the time is come to make a new creation: from the vault of heaven bring him up, out of Seir draw him forth, that he may make his voice heard to us in Lebanon, a second time by the hand of Yinnon [a rabbinical name of Messiah derived from Psalm 72:17].*[2]

From Ha-Kallir's prayer, it is obvious that the Jewish people of that era believed the Messiah had already come and were praying that He may come "a second time." Some of the medieval scholars who interpreted this passage in an individual sense applied it either to

Jeremiah or to Isaiah. Others applied it to Hezekiah; and still others, to any righteous person who suffers innocently.

THE TWO-MESSIAH THEORY

Many of the ancient rabbis were aware of the seemingly divergent elements in the Messianic prophecies. Whereas some prophecies spoke of the suffering Messiah (Isa. 50:5–7; 53), others described a triumphant Messiah who will subdue the rebellious nations and establish His Kingdom (Ps. 2; 110). To resolve this problem, the rabbis resorted to the theory of two Messiahs: *the suffering Messiah,* called Messiah ben Joseph, who dies in battle against Edom (Rome); followed by *the triumphant Messiah,* Messiah ben David, who establishes His Kingdom of righteousness after defeating the Gentile nations.[3]

Another attempt to resolve the seeming contradiction of both a suffering and triumphant Messiah is mentioned in Pesikta Rabbathi. According to this theory, the Messiah ben David suffers in every generation for the sins of each generation. Other rabbinical authorities sought to find a solution to this puzzle in various ingenious ways, which, however, did not commend them to most Jewish people.

Some rabbinical authorities have postponed the solution of this and all other perplexing questions until the coming of the prophet Elijah, the forerunner of the Messiah, who will make all things clear.[4]

In the New Testament, this apparent contradiction is resolved by the doctrine concerning the First Advent of the suffering Christ followed by His triumphant Second Coming (Mt. 23:29; Jn. 14:3; Acts 1:11; 1 Th. 4:14–17).

The chief representative of the non-Messianic, collective interpretation was the 11th-century French-Jewish scholar, Rabbi Shlomo Itzhaki (1040–1105), best known by his initials as Rashi. Rashi's views on Isaiah 53 were later supported by the famous commentators and scholars Joseph Kimchi (1105–70) and his son, David (1160–1235), and later by the renowned Jewish scholar and diplomat, Don Isaac Abarbanel of Spain (1437–1508).

In time the non-Messianic interpretation of Isaiah 53 practically became an official dogma among most Jewish people. Nevertheless, many learned rabbis have continued

to object strenuously to this interpretation as doing violence to the literal and obvious sense of Isaiah 53. Thus Rabbi Moshe Kohen ibn Crispin (13th century) complained bitterly that those who interpret Isaiah 53 as referring to Israel do violence to it and to its natural meaning, having "inclined after the stubbornness of their own hearts and their own opinion." He continued:

I'm pleased to interpret the Parasha [passage] in accordance with the teaching of our rabbis, of the King Messiah . . . and adhere to the literal sense.

Thus I shall be free from forced and farfetched inter-pretations of which others are guilty.[5]

Similar opinions were voiced later by other prominent rabbinical authorities. However, the collective interpretation of Isaiah 53 remains the dominant one today among the majority of Jewish people. Strangely enough, many liberal Christian theologians, whom Old Testament scholar Franz Delitzsch once called "the uncircumcised rabbis," have supported the Jewish position, sometimes out of deference to their Jewish friends or because it fell in line with their own liberal views, which had no place for the suffering Messiah predicted by the prophets.

JEWISH PROBLEMS
WITH MESSIAH'S DEITY

Jewish arguments against the Christian interpretation of Isaiah 53 are generally based on a misinterpretation of Christian doctrine concerning the humanity and deity of Christ, that is, the doctrine of the Incarnation. The Jewish controversialists contrasted the infinite majesty and omnipotence of the eternal God with the physical limitations of Jesus while He was on Earth in the form of a frail human being.

Here are some typical Jewish arguments against the divine nature of Christ:

1. Behold, my servant (52:13).

If Christ is God, how can He also be called a servant?

2. He shall be exalted (52:13).

How can it be said of God that He will be exalted (future tense)?

Is not God always exalted?

3. Smitten of God, and afflicted (53:4).

If Christ is God, how can He be smitten and afflicted by God?

4. And the LORD hath laid on him the iniquity of us all (53:6).

If the Lord has laid on Him all our iniquity, then Jesus must be inferior to the Lord.

5. And he made his grave with the wicked (53:9).

How can God die and be buried?

6. And the pleasure of the LORD shall prosper in his hand (53:10).

If Jesus is God, how can it be said of Him, "the pleasure of the LORD shall prosper in his hand?"

These and many more such objections completely ignore the basic New Testament view of the Incarnation, expressed so poignantly by the apostle Paul:

Let this mind be in you, which was also in Christ Jesus, Who being in the form of God, thought it not robbery [literally, "a thing to be held on to"] to be equal with God, But made himself of no reputation, and took upon him the form of a servant, and was made in the likeness of men; And, being found in fashion as a man, he humbled himself and became obedient unto death, even the death of the cross (Phil. 2:5–8).

By ignoring the New Testament doctrine of the Incarnation, Jewish scholars have sought to make the Christian interpretation of Isaiah 53 and other Messianic prophecies appear untenable or even nonsensical.

The famous Rabbi Manasseh ben Israel of Amsterdam (1604–57), who successfully persuaded British leader Oliver Cromwell to readmit Jewish people to England in 1655, wrote a paraphrase and a commentary in which he presented the popular Jewish position on Isaiah 52:13—53:12, stating that the Gentiles will one day confess that it was the Jews who suffered innocently for the sins of the Gentile nations.

> "HE HUMBLED HIMSELF AND BECAME OBEDIENT UNTO DEATH."

RABBI MANASSEH BEN ISRAEL'S PARAPHRASE OF ISAIAH 53:

52:13 Behold my servant Israel shall understand: he shall be exalted, extolled, and raised very high, at the coming of the Messiah.

52:14 As many of the nations were astonished at thee, O Israel, saying at the time of the captivity, Truly he is disfigured above all mankind in his countenance and form:

52:15 So at that time they shall speak of thy grandeur; even kings themselves shall shut their mouths in astonishment: for what They had never been told they shall see, and what they had not heard they shall understand.

53:1   Who would have believed (the nations will say) what we see, had it been related to them? And look upon what a vile nation the arm of the Lord has manifested itself.

53:2   He came up miraculously as a branch and a root out of a dry ground, for he had no form nor comeliness: we saw him, but so hideous, that it did not seem to us an appearance, for which we should envy him.

53:3   He was despised and rejected from the society of men, a man of sorrows, accustomed to suffer troubles; we hid our faces from him, he was despised and unesteemed among us.

53:4   But now we see that the sickness and troubles which we ought in reason to have suffered, he suffered and endured, and we thought that he was justly smitten by God and afflicted.

53:5   Whereas he suffered the sicknesses and sufferings which we deserved for our sins; he bore the chastisement which our peace and felicity deserved; but his troubles appear to have been the cure of ourselves.

53:6 All we like sheep went astray: we followed every one his own sect, and so the Lord seems to have transferred on him the punishment of us all.

53:7 He was oppressed and afflicted: he was taken by us as a lamb to the slaughter and as a sheep before its shearers, depriving him of life and property: and he was dumb and opened not his mouth.

53:8 From prison and these torments he is now delivered: and who would have thought of this his happy age when he was banished from the holy land? Through the wickedness of my people (each nation will say) this blow came upon them.

53:9 He was buried with malefactors, and suffered various torments with the rich, without having committed crime or used deceit with his mouth.

53:10 But it was the Lord (the Prophet says) who wished to make him sick and afflict him,

> "HE WAS DESPISED. . . AND UNESTEEMED AMONG US."

in order to purify him: if he offer his soul as an expiation he shall see seed, he shall prolong his days, and the will and determination of the Lord shall prosper in his hand. **53:11** For the trouble which his soul suffered in captivity, he shall see good, shall be satisfied with days: by his wisdom my righteous servant Israel shall justify the many, and he will bear their burdens.

53:12 Therefore I will give him his share of spoil among the many and powerful of Gog and Magog, because he gave himself up unto death for the sanctification of my name; and was numbered with the transgressors; and he bore the offense of many, even praying for the very transgressors from whom he received injuries.[6]

This paraphrase is most interesting for it shows clearly the self-righteousness and self-infatuation of the rabbis who taught that Israel is completely righteous and suffers innocently merely because of Gentile wickedness. Rabbi Manasseh, commenting further on his paraphrase of Isaiah 53:6, explained:

> ***But all we like sheep went astray,*** *etc. That is, they [the Gentiles] will not only acknowledge the*

*ill-treatment and bodily inflictions they had made Israel suffer, but at the same time their errors, attributing their wickedness thereto; for many will say, we all (Ishmaelites and Edumeans), [in rabbinical parlance, they are the Mahomedans and the Christians] like sheep went astray, each in his own way followed a new sect; just as the prophet Jeremiah says (16:19). **And the Lord made to fall on him, [on Israel] the wickedness of us all.** That is, we [the Gentiles] erred, they followed the truth; consequently they suffered the punishments, which we deserved. We deprived them of their property as tribute, and afflicted their bodies with various kinds of torture, **yet he opened not his mouth,** etc. The experience of this is seen every day, particularly in the cruelties of the Inquisition, and the false testimony raised against them to take their wool and rob them of their property.[7]*

It would be difficult to conceive of a greater misinterpretation of the text or distortion of the obvious sense of the disputed passage.

THE DIVISION OF
ISAIAH 52:13—53:12

Having considered the differing Jewish and Christian interpretations of Isaiah 53, we shall now translate the Hebrew text and seek to interpret its natural and obvious sense.

The passage may be divided into five sections, each consisting of three verses.

Section One: Isaiah 52:13–15

Jehovah introduces His faithful servant and announces that he will accomplish the divine purpose and shall, in the future, be highly exalted.

Section Two: Isaiah 53:1–3

Penitent Israel's confession.

Section Three: Isaiah 53:4–6

Jehovah's servant suffers for the sins of his people.

Section Four: Isaiah 53:7–9

Although without sin, the servant submits himself to humiliation, suffering, and death without opening his mouth.

Section Five: Isaiah 53:10–12

The servant's offering was God-ordained in order to bring forgiveness and redemption to many. Yet the servant shall rise from the dead, have a lasting following, and rejoice in the results of his completed work.

The heart of the issue in this hotly contested passage is the question of whether the prophet considered Israel to be Jehovah's servant, as most modern Jews and liberal Christians do, or whether the

> THE SERVANT'S OFFERING WAS GOD-ORDAINED IN ORDER TO BRING FORGIVENESS AND REDEMPTION TO MANY.

prophet gave us a word portrait of a God-appointed individual who suffers innocently for the sins of his people, just as the oldest Jewish tradition and the early church have always maintained.

It is obvious that only the second position is consistent with the common-sense meaning of the text. Repeatedly, the prophet refers to Jehovah's servant in the singular: "he," "him," "his," or "thee." Furthermore, the prophet's portrait of the servant is utterly irreconcilable with Isaiah's frequently expressed scathing opinions about Israel.

Whereas Israel is castigated as a blind and disobedient servant (Isa. 24:18–20) who refuses to obey the Law (Isa. 42:24), the servant of the Lord is presented as humble and silent under extreme suffering and torture (Isa. 53:7). The Jewish people have always protested loudly against their tormentors. Whatever Israel's virtues may be, silence under suffering was never one of them.

We shall see in greater detail the essential differences between Israel as a servant and the suffering servant of God—the Messiah of Isaiah 53.

It is clear that in this great prophecy, Israel is not the innocent sufferer for the redemption of the nations but is herself the object of salvation through God's servant. This remarkable chapter compels us to reflect on the life and destiny of Jesus in the light of the New Testament. However, as soon as we try to force it to fit Israel as a people, the comparison falls apart.

Because of the striking parallel between the suffering Messiah of this amazing prophecy and the prophecy's remarkable fulfillment in the person of Jesus, Isaiah 53 has been excluded from the Sabbath readings of the Prophets (the Haftorah) in the synagogue. Some have called Isaiah 53 "the secret chapter" or "the guilty conscience of the synagogue."

The 13th-century rabbinical scholar, Rabbi Moshe Kohen ibn Crispin, probably most clearly enunciated the traditional Messianic interpretation of Isaiah 53:

This prophecy was delivered by Isaiah at the divine command for the purpose of making known to us something about the nature of the future Messiah, who is to come and deliver Israel . . . in order that if any one should arise claiming to be himself the Messiah, we may reflect, and look to see whether we can observe in him any resemblance to the traits described here: if there is any such resemblance, then we may believe that he is the Messiah our righteousness; but if not, we cannot do so.[8]

II.

JEHOVAH INTRODUCES HIS SERVANT

SECTION ONE: ISAIAH 52:13–15

ᴨ **Bible Text** ᴨ

52:13 *Behold my servant shall deal wisely, He shall be lifted up, he shall be exalted and shall be very high.*

52:14 *Even as many were appalled at thee, So marred was his figure beyond any man's, And his form from that of the sons of men,*

52:15 *So shall he sprinkle many nations, Kings shall shut their mouths before him, Because that which has not been told to them, they shall see, And that which they never heard, they shall comprehend.*

▪ Comment ▪

In this section, which is a prelude to the prophecy of Isaiah 53, Jehovah Himself introduces His servant, the Messiah.

Verse 13: *Behold* (Hebrew: *hinneh* or *hen*). This is the prophet's favorite exclamation when he draws attention to a matter of great importance.

Behold my servant. As we already have seen, the crux of the dispute between Jewish and Christian commentators revolves around the question, Who is the servant? Is it Israel, as most contemporary Jewish scholars (and many liberal Christian ones) insist, or does the prophet visualize a God-appointed individual who willingly takes on himself the sins of his people and dies for them in order to redeem them? We have seen that this passage cannot be applied to Israel as a nation or to ideal Israel because (1) the prophecy clearly refers to an individual and (2) the portrait drawn by the prophet is

> ▪
> WHEN WE COMPARE
> ISAIAH 53 WITH THE
> LIFE OF JESUS, THE
> PROPHECY SPRINGS
> TO LIFE.
> ▪

incompatible with historical Israel and with Isaiah's opinion of this people.

However, when we compare Isaiah 53 with the life of Jesus, the prophecy springs to life and takes on the reality of a historical personality. Nevertheless, a genuine link does exist between national Israel and the suffering servant of God. Both Israel and her Messiah were called to be God's servants. Israel failed to accomplish her divine mission, whereas the Messiah, God's obedient servant, accomplished the mission the Father entrusted to Him.

Furthermore, God's suffering servant personified what Israel was intended to be: "a light to lighten the Gentiles" (Lk. 2:32; cf. Isa. 49:6). Thus, in a sense, Israel and her Messiah are one.

Shall deal wisely. The King James Version (KJV) translates this phrase as "shall prosper." The Hebrew verb *yaskil* means "to act wisely or prudently." Thus "to prosper" is the result of wise or prudent action.

He shall be lifted up, he shall be exalted and shall be very high. Three verbs are used to convey the absolute height to which the servant of God shall attain. It will be absolute, beyond all comparison.

The first two verbs, *lifted up* and *exalted,* are the same as Isaiah used about the Lord whom he saw sitting on the throne, "high and exalted [lifted up]" (Hebrew: *ram ve-nissa,* Isa. 6:1).

Verse 14: *Even as many were appalled at thee.* Jehovah addresses Himself directly to His servant in the pronoun of the second person as "thee." The word *appalled* (Hebrew: *shamem*) means "devastated." It expresses deep, bewildered amazement at the transformation of the servant's once marred and distorted visage (beyond human resemblance) to the now exalted personage.

So marred was his figure beyond any man's. This is a parenthetical sentence in which the prophet explains why so many were appalled at His appearance. We have here a glimpse into the depth of the Messiah's intense suffering, which transfigured His entire image beyond human semblance.

Verse 15: *So shall he sprinkle many nations.* Here the prophet compares the servant's previous physical appearance, which was marred and distorted, to His exalted, high-priestly position as the one who cleanses many from the defilement of their sins. "To sprinkle" (Hebrew: *yazzeh,* from the verb *nizeh,* "to sprinkle" or "to be sprinkled") is often used in the Old Testament to describe a leper's ritual cleansing by the sprinkling of the blood of a sacrifice (Lev. 14:7), or the veil in the Tabernacle (Lev. 4:6).

Interestingly, in the Talmud, one of Messiah's names is Nagua—"the leprous one" (Sanhedrin 98b). This name is based on Isaiah 53:4 and 8. Jehovah's servant, once shunned like a leper, now brings cleansing to the nations—not through the blood of animals but by His own blood.

Some Jewish interpreters, such as Dr. Israel Slotki, translate *yazzeh* not as "sprinkle" but "startle." This translation is possible; but "sprinkle" is more suitable because of the content and the other passages where this verb is also so translated (Lev. 4:6; 14:7).

Kings shall shut their mouths before him. The convincing and convicting force of the Messiah's message shall be so immense that the great among men will stand before Him in mute awe and reverence because what they will hear from His lips was never heard before; and the matchless life they will see was never seen before. This concept is described elsewhere in Isaiah:

Kings shall see and arise, Princes they shall worship, Because of Jehovah, who is faithful, And the Holy One of Israel who has chosen thee (49:7).

Isaiah 52:13–15 forms a prologue to the great Messianic vision of chapter 53 and sums up its entire message.

III.

THE CONFESSION OF A PENITENT PEOPLE

SECTION TWO: ISAIAH 53:1–3
n **Bible Text** n

53:1   *Who has believed the message that we have heard? And the arm of the LORD, to whom was it revealed?*

53:2   *For he grew up like a tender plant before him, And as a root out of a dry ground, He had no form nor beauty, And when we looked at him, there was no attractive appearance, That we should desire him.*

53:3   *He was despised and shunned by men, A man of afflictions and acquainted with suffering, He was as one from whom men hide their face, He was despised and we esteemed him not.*

■ Comment ■

Verse 1: *Who has believed the message that we have heard?* It is essential that we understand who is asking the question.

The majority of modern Jewish interpreters (and some non-Jewish ones) put the question in the mouths of the Gentile nations who, in the last days, will see the exaltation of the once-despised Jewish people.

Although most flattering to the national ego, this interpretation is inconsistent with both the prophet's known views about his people and the language of his prophecy.

Repeatedly, the prophet denounced his people for being deaf and blind to the will of their God (42:19–20; 43:24).

According to Isaiah, the children of Israel do not deserve the name Israel, and their allegiance to Jehovah is insincere (48:1). He characterized his nation as "an obstinate people with a neck like an iron sinew and their forehead is like brass" (48:4).

Israel's entire history and national character are completely out of harmony with the prophet's portrait of God's obedient servant, who takes upon Himself the sins of His people to redeem all men. Thus the only reasonable answer regarding who posed the question, "Who has believed the message we have heard?" is that it is asked by repentant Israel or by a remnant of godly Jewish people when they finally recognize their past rebellion against God and His servant, the Messiah. In reality, the sense of the question is the people's self-accusation, stating that so few of them have believed.

The word translated "our report" (Hebrew: *shmuatenu*) literally means "that which we have heard" or "our message." It refers to the cumulative witness of the prophets who, for many generations, prophesied about the coming of the divinely appointed Savior to deliver His people from their sins.

And the arm of the LORD, to whom was it revealed? "The arm of the LORD" is a figure that describes God's power and wisdom as manifested in His redemptive acts in history.

Verse 2: *For he grew up like a tender plant before him.* Isaiah points to the unpretentious and humble beginnings of the servant, who was like a tender plant bursting forth from the dry ground. The Hebrew word for "root" is *yonek,* meaning "a suckling" or, horticulturally speaking, "a twig" or "a stalk."

In 11:1 the prophet proclaimed, "There shall come forth a shoot From the root stock of Jesse, And a twig out of his roots shall bear fruit."

The connection between the Messiah proclaimed in the first part of Isaiah and God's suffering servant in the second part is strongly suggested here.

And as a root. In the prophetic writings, the Messiah is often called a root or branch. This is a reference to his Davidic descent (Isa. 11:10).

Out of a dry ground (Hebrew: *me-eretz tziah*). Under Herod, the Davidic dynasty became all but extinct. The attrition of time and the murderous jealousy of Herod, so-called the Great, almost wiped out all known or potential claimants to the throne of David. In this sense, "the root of Jesse" vegetated and finally sprung up in "dry ground."

Spiritually speaking, Israel in the first century before Christ and long after became "a dry land." No longer were there prophets to proclaim to Israel the will and the Word of Jehovah. It was the age of the great pharisaic scholars, legislators, and interpreters of the Law of Moses who taught according to their own human understanding. It was the age of Jewish scholasticism— acute, occasionally even brilliant, but not very creative spiritually. It was an age somewhat reminiscent of the later medieval scholasticism of the church.

Eretz tziah, "a dry land," may originally have suggested the name Zion, which means "a dry hill or place." This interpretation would point to the fact that the grandeur of Zion and all it represents was not inherent in the land itself, which was dry and barren, but came from God, who has chosen Zion as His habitation.

And when we looked at him, there was no attractive appearance, That we should desire him. Nothing in the outward circumstances of the servant's advent made him attractive to his people or to the world. He arrived with no pomp or circumstance and no earthly splendor usually attending the arrival of earthly princelings. He arrived with nothing to excite the imagination of His countrymen or of the world. Israel's vision of the Messiah was focused on his majestic appearance as a king and conqueror who would subdue Israel's enemies, impose his peace on the nations, and establish his and Israel's glorious Kingdom. Foremost in Jewish minds were those passages of Scripture that predicted divine judgment involving the downfall of the Gentiles and the establishment of a Kingdom where

> *The wolf shall dwell with the lamb, And the calf and the young lion shall lie down together, They shall no longer hurt nor destroy in my holy mountain. For the earth shall be filled with the knowledge of God As the waters cover the sea. And the root of Jesse shall stand for a standard for the nations* (Isa. 11:5, 10; 65:22–25).

Isaiah's MESSIAH

These ideas have always exercised an enormous fascination for the Jewish people. They formed Israel's "vision splendid," which she transmitted to all mankind. However, there was scant recognition of the fact that, before this Messianic Kingdom could become a reality, the Messiah must first suffer, die, and rise again from the dead. This aspect of the Messianic mission hardly registered on Israel's national consciousness. Nor did the nation ever become deeply aware of the fact that Messiah's mission was to bring His people and the nations to repentance and to faith in Him as the divinely appointed Redeemer.

It was with these truths in mind that the risen Christ, on the way to Emmaus, chided the two disciples:

O foolish ones, and slow of heart to believe all that the prophets have spoken! Ought not Christ [Messiah] have

THE CONFESSION OF A PENITENT PEOPLE

suffered these things, and to enter into his glory? And beginning at Moses and all the prophets, he expounded unto them, in all the scriptures, the things concerning himself (Lk. 24:25–27).

A Messiah without earthly splendor, humble and humiliated, who is tormented and dies on a shameful cross as a vicarious and voluntary sacrifice for the redemption of Israel and mankind, has always been and still remains offensive to Jewish thinking.

Verse 3: *He was despised and shunned by men.* In earlier rabbinic literature, the Messiah was recognized, at least in part, as a sufferer. The Jewish prayer book frequently alludes to Isaiah 53 and to Messiah's suffering; but later, contemporary Judaism sought to eliminate, or at least to play down, all such allusions to a suffering Savior.

The legend of the two Messiahs was invented in an effort to reconcile the two biblical strands of thought: one that speaks of a suffering Messiah and the other that foresees his victorious reign. One is Messiah ben Ephraim (also called Messiah ben Joseph). He is the suffering Messiah who dies in battle against Armilius (Rome). Then comes the second Messiah, Messiah ben David, who is victorious over Rome (all pagan powers), restores the kingdom of Israel, and establishes peace among the nations of the world.[9] Such was the feeble effort to reconcile the two distinct, biblical strands of prophecy: the First Coming of the Savior as "the Lamb of God" who sacrifices Himself for the redemption of all men, and His Second Coming as King of kings to establish His glorious Kingdom.

> A MESSIAH . . . WHO IS TORMENTED AND DIES . . . REMAINS OFFENSIVE TO JEWISH THINKING.

The prophet, by inspiration and also from knowledge of his own people, foresaw all this truth and spoke of the servant as already despised and rejected by men. The Hebrew word for "men" is *shim,* the poetic form for the regular *anashim,* a reference not to the ordinary rank-and-file men (*hoi polloi*), but to men of stature. Such men shunned Jesus. The very fact that He came from humble origins and dwelt in Nazareth, an obscure Galilean town not even mentioned in rabbinical literature, was, in the eyes of His contemporaries, an almost insurmountable obstacle (Jn. 1:46; 7:41).

A man of afflictions and acquainted with suffering. We translated the Hebrew word *machoboth* as "afflictions," which is nearer to the original than the KJV's "grief." The afflictions could be either physical or spiritual.

Jewish controversialists have maintained that, since Jesus never suffered personal affliction during His lifetime nor was ever sick Himself, those particular words could not apply to Him. However, this is not a reasonable argument. Like all the prophets, Jesus identified Himself with His people. He was afflicted in their afflictions and felt all His people's maladies with a keen, personal sensitivity, even as Isaiah did centuries before:

> *From the sole of the foot even to the head, There is not a sound spot, Only wounds and bruises and running sores, Which have not been pressed out nor bound up, Nor softened with oil* (1:6).

The servant came to suffer with and for His people and to lay down His life for them.

He was as one from whom men hide their face, He was despised and we esteemed him not. People are loathe to look at a man whom they hate immensely; and in all the history of Israel, no other was more intensely hated and despised than the person of the servant of God. The prophet rightly called him "a man of affliction and acquainted with suffering." For hundreds of years, His name was not even mentioned among the Jewish people except by such circumlocutions as "that man" or "the hanged one." The words *he was despised* are repeated twice in this sentence to emphasize their intensity. Jesus' Hebrew name, *Yeshua* (Savior), has been deliberately distorted into *Yeshu,* the initial letters of which were supposed to spell out a Hebrew sentence that means, "Let his name and his memory be blotted out." This aversion to Him even increased with the passing of time.[9] However, with the growing social, moral, and religious ferment among the Jewish people, their attitude is gradually becoming more positive.

IV.

THE VICARIOUS SUFFERING OF JEHOVAH'S SERVANT

SECTION THREE: ISAIAH 53:4–6
ⁿ Bible Text ⁿ

53:4   *And yet he surely did bear our diseases, And our afflictions he did carry. But we considered him stricken, Smitten of God and afflicted.*

53:5   *But he was wounded for our transgressions, He was crushed for our iniquities, The chastisement that secured our peace was upon him, And by his stripes, healing has come to us.*

53:6   *All we have gone astray like sheep, Every one of us turned to his own way, But the LORD caused to fall on him The iniquity of us all.*

■ Comment ■

Verse 4: *And yet he surely did bear our diseases, And our afflictions he did carry.* Repentant Israel continues its great confession as it looks on God's servant, the nation's once-despised Messiah. Now the children of Israel acknowledge that He did not suffer for His own sins but that He carried on His shoulders the burden of their sins and the pain of their transgressions. His suffering was expiatory and vicarious in nature. The word *nasa,* meaning "bear," is also used in connection with the sacrifices of expiation (Lev. 5:1, 17; 16:22; 20:19, 20).

But we considered him stricken, smitten of God and afflicted. Three expressions are used here. "Stricken" (Hebrew: *nagua*) refers to a loathsome disease, such as leprosy; "smitten of God," a divine retribution for a heinous sin; and "afflicted," as one might be afflicted by the punishment for one's crime. All describe the terrible consequences of sin. The Talmud calls Jesus a transgressor; and the renowned 12th-century Jewish scholar, Maimonides, claimed Jesus deserved the violent death He suffered.

Verse 5: *But he was wounded for our transgressions, He was crushed for our iniquities.* "But he" is the emphatic assertion that the real cause of the servant's suffering was not, as Israel falsely assumed, for His own sins but, rather, for the transgressions of His people. The word *wounded* (Hebrew: *mecholal*) literally means "he was pierced." Only an inspired prophet could use a word that so literally corresponds to what actually happened to God's righteous servant, the Messiah Jesus. The phrases *wounded* (or *pierced*) *for our transgressions* and *crushed for our iniquities* express fully the vicarious nature of the suffering of God's servant—the innocent for the guilty.

Despite the assertions of the rabbis and some non-Jewish theologians that vicarious suffering is morally objectionable and unacceptable, it is, nevertheless, exactly what the Scriptures teach. It also is what history and life itself teach.

The entire sacrificial system symbolizes substitution of the innocent for the guilty. No sacrificial animal, however perfect, could, by itself, make atonement for sin. In the last analysis, the sacrifice was merely symbolic and pointed to the fact that the sinner deserved to die and that it was God's servant who voluntarily took on Himself the sins of all men. This is why John the Baptist pointed to Jesus as "the Lamb of God, who taketh away the sins of the world" (Jn. 1:29).

> BY THE SERVANT'S VICARIOUS SUFFERING, WE MAY SECURE PEACE—*SHALOM*.

Sin brings in its wake suffering and death, not only on the sinner, but frequently on the innocent as well, just as the voluntary sacrifice of an "innocent" person may bring healing and salvation to the guilty.

The chastisement that secured our peace was upon him (*musar shlomenu,* the "chastisement that secured peace"). Forgiveness, to be genuine, must be obtained at a price. In order to forgive sinners, a righteous God must base that forgiveness on moral ground. Otherwise, forgiveness would be morally objectionable and spiritually meaningless because there would be no difference between righteousness and wickedness. But God is not only merciful but also righteous. So God's righteous servant took on Himself the chastisement, or punishment, that secures our peace.

And by his stripes, healing has come to us. This line complements the preceding one. "By his stripes," that is, by the servant's vicarious suffering, we may secure peace—*shalom*—that is, complete reconciliation with God, harmony within our souls, and peace with men. Healing in this context is primarily the healing of the soul from the sickness of sin. Yet, in addition to spiritual healing, physical and emotional healing may be included.

In our age it is recognized that physical ailments frequently have emotional or psychic foundations. Our hospitals often overflow with such patients. The servant who brings sinful people peace with God and healing to their souls also brings healing from a multitude of diseases.

Verse 6: *All we have gone astray like sheep.* "All we" (Hebrew: *kullanu*) is an emphatic assertion concerning all people, without exception. It means that every human being alive has an innate bent to stray or wander away from the path of righteousness. Straying is characteristic of sheep.

Every one of us turned to his own way. The emphasis here is on "his own way"—not God's way. Sheep are not accountable for wandering off and becoming lost, because they have no understanding or judgment. But when people who are endowed with God-given minds and consciences behave like sheep, they cannot be held blameless. They are committing sin.

But the Lord caused to fall on him the iniquity of us all. People are, by nature, inclined to wander off like sheep, going their own ways even though doing so may lead them to destruction. Yet God in His mercy has appointed His righteous servant, the Good Shepherd, to guide them to the path of life.

V.

THE ORDEAL AND DEATH OF JEHOVAH'S SERVANT

SECTION FOUR: ISAIAH 53:7–9
ᴨ **Bible Text** ᴨ

53:7 *He was tormented and he submitted himself, And opened not his mouth. As a lamb that is led to the slaughter, And as a ewe sheep before her shearers is dumb, So he also opened not his mouth.*

53:8 *From prison and from judgment he was removed, Yet who of his generation pondered this? That he was cut off from the land of the living, For the transgression of my people the stroke fell upon him.*

53:9 *And his grave was appointed with the wicked, And with a rich man in his death, Although he had committed no violence, Neither was there any deception in his mouth.*

▨ Comment ▨

Verse 7: *He was tormented and he submitted himself.* Our translation differs from the KJV, which reads, "He was oppressed and he was afflicted." We believe that our translation comes closer to the original text. The entire sense of this sentence stresses the voluntary, humble, and quiet submission of the ill-treated servant of God to His tormentors.

> WHENEVER THE JEWISH PEOPLE WERE ABLE, THEY RESISTED [THEIR TORMENTORS] WITH ALL THEIR MIGHT

And opened not his mouth. This prediction harmonizes with the story of Jesus' trial and His silence before His accusers (Mt. 26:62–63; 27:12).

As a lamb that is led to the slaughter. The New Testament references to Jesus as the Lamb of God have their roots in the story of the Passover lamb and the sprinkling of its blood on the doorposts of the Israelite households in Egypt (Ex. 12:3–4, 7). They also refer to the Messiah's lamb-like submission to His tormentors and to His sacrifice.

This kind of submissive behavior can in no way be attributed to Israel as a nation. Whatever Israel's virtues are, suffering in silence and submission to her tormentors is not one of them. Whenever the Jewish people were able, they resisted with all their might; and when they were unable, they protested vigorously and vociferously against their oppressors. In fact, they never considered suffering in silence as a virtue. Even in the infamous Nazi extermination camps and ghettos, they resisted whenever they were able or sent messages of protest and alarm to the rest of the world. This reaction was understandable and natural on their part; but it is, nevertheless, completely at odds with the description in Isaiah 53 of the behavior of God's servant.

Verse 8: *He was removed from prison and from judgment.* "From prison" (Hebrew: *me-otzer*) means a place of restraint or imprisonment. One marvels at the accuracy of the prophecy in so many details when compared with the events described in the Gospels in connection with Jesus' death.

Yet who of his generation pondered this? Jesus' contemporaries gave little thought to the importance of His death. Life went on as before. Probably too many events were taking place during that turbulent period in Israel's history for anyone to ponder too much about the significance of the death of an unknown Galilean teacher. Only some of His disciples and a number of His other followers believed in His subsequent resurrection. Yet Jesus' coming, death, and resurrection were the most important events in the history of mankind. Since then, world history has been divided into two epochs: B.C., before Christ; and A.D., *Anno Domini*, the year of our Lord Jesus Christ.

That he was cut off from the land of the living. His life was cut off prematurely. He lived a short life, about 33 years. With the crucifixion, Jesus' earthly career came to an end—or so His adversaries had hoped. But in fact, His impact on mankind had only begun. He lives on in the minds and hearts of countless millions. He cannot be erased from the consciousness of men. His Truth goes marching on.

Well did Jesus say, "And I, if I be lifted up from the earth, will draw all men unto me" (Jn. 12:32).

For the transgression of my people the stroke fell upon him. Jewish interpreters put these words and the rest of Isaiah 53 into the mouths of the Gentile nations, whom they say will realize one day that the Jewish people suffered innocently all along and voluntarily took the punishment that was due each of them.

To bolster their argument, they maintain that the words *upon him* are plural in Hebrew (*lamo*), meaning "upon them." The regular singular "upon him" should be *lo* (*lamed vav*). Yet, in actuality, *lamo* is used repeatedly both as a plural and as a singular (Job 20:23; 22:2). "He makes it a graven image and falls down before it [*lamo*]" (Isa. 44:15). The argument is specious.

The term *my people* can only refer to Israel, for whom God's righteous servant suffers and dies.

Verse 9: ***And his grave was appointed with the wicked, And with a rich man in his death.*** Again we are astounded at the accuracy of the prophetic prediction, which found its fulfillment in the events of the crucifixion. Jesus' body, considered by Jewish and Roman authorities to be that of a rebel, normally would have been assigned with the two criminals who died on the other two crosses; and, had it not been for divine intervention, it would have been buried where criminals usually were buried, in an unmarked grave. "The rich man," Joseph of Arimathea (Mt. 27:57), intervened with the Roman authorities and had Jesus buried in a private grave in his garden, "wherein never man before was laid" (Lk. 23:53).

Although he had committed no violence. The complete innocence of the servant, who committed no crime in deed or in word, is emphasized here. Nothing in Jesus' life justified such a cruel and extreme sentence.

VI.

THE FUTURE GLORY OF JEHOVAH'S SERVANT

SECTION FIVE: ISAIAH 53:10–12
n **Bible Text** n

53:10   *Yet it pleased the LORD to crush him, To afflict him with grief, If his soul shall make a trespass offering, He shall see seed, prolong his days, And the purpose of the LORD shall prosper in his hand.*

53:11   *He shall see of the travail of his soul and shall be satisfied. By his knowledge shall my righteous servant justify many, And their iniquities he shall bear.*

53:12 *Therefore will I give him a portion among the great, And with the strong will he divide spoil; Because he poured out his life unto death, And was numbered among the transgressors. Yet he bore the sin of many, And made intercession for the transgressors.*

ⁿ Comment ⁿ

Verse 10: *Yet it pleased the LORD to crush him.* All that happened to Jehovah's servant was, in the final analysis, the result of Jehovah's will. It was Jehovah's will to crush Him; it was His will to afflict Him with "grief," which, in Hebrew (*hechli*), is the same word used in verses 3 and 4.

If his soul shall make a trespass offering. Asham is a "trespass offering," distinct from every other sacrifice. It was made by individuals to compensate for any wrong they committed. It discharged them from guilt and set them free (Lev. 5:15). The central idea of the trespass offering was satisfaction demanded by a just God.

Thus God's servant made Himself a sacrifice in restitution for the sins of every man, woman, and child, individually.

He shall see seed, prolong his days. "He shall see seed" refers to those who are redeemed by His sacrifice. "He shall prolong his days" refers to His resurrection and the life that only began after His crucifixion. Jewish commentators have maintained that "seed" refers exclusively to physical offspring, that is, children; but in reality, it refers also to spiritual seed, a following (Ps. 22:30; Isa. 65:25; Mal. 2:15).

And the purpose of the LORD shall prosper in his hand. It was the whole counsel of God, which the servant accomplished, because of His willingness to offer Himself as a trespass offering. This purpose of God's continues to prosper through the ages. Jehovah's servant was appointed to restore Israel so the nation might, in the end, become a light to the world and carry God's salvation to the ends of the earth (Isa. 49:6).

Verse 11: ***He shall see of the travail of his soul and shall be satisfied.*** The servant shall look on His travail and

> "HE BORE THE SIN OF MANY AND MADE INTERCESSION FOR THE TRANSGRESSORS."

the sorrows His earthly life brought Him, and He will be well satisfied with the results of His sacrifice.

By his knowledge shall my righteous servant justify many. "My righteous servant" is used here in an emphatic form to express the absolute righteousness of God's chosen servant. Through the knowledge of Him, others were made righteous. The knowledge of Him is not just mental but involves experiencing a living, on-going, and personal relationship with God's servant, the Messiah. It is justification by faith in Him.

And their iniquities he shall bear. This action goes beyond the Messiah's finished work and points to His continuous work of mediation (Heb. 8:6).

Verse 12: ***Therefore will I give him a portion among the great.*** *Barabim* means "among the great ones" and also "among many." Here the prophet further elaborates the thought in Isaiah 52:15: "So also shall he sprinkle many nations, Kings shall shut their mouths before him."

The completed work of Jehovah's servant will affect not only Israel but also the nations of the world. (See Isa. 49:7.) The prophet foresees the time when the great men of history shall pay homage to God's servant, the Messiah.

Because he poured out his life unto death. His impact on the nations and the homage that the mighty and great will pay Him will be the consequence of His having poured out His life, although at the time of His crucifixion, those who sat in judgment over Him considered Him a transgressor.

Yet he bore the sin of many. Far from being a transgressor, God's servant was the Savior of transgressors and interceded for them at the very moment they were putting Him to death (Lk. 23:34).

THE FUTURE GLORY OF JEHOVAH'S SERVANT

CONCLUSION

With Chapter 53, which is the heart and center of the Book of Consolation, Messianic prophecy reaches its majestic pinnacle.

Franz Delitzsch, to whom all who ever commented on Isaiah in the course of the last century owe a great debt, wrote the following in his commentary:

The Servant of Jehovah goes through shame to glory and through death to life. He conquers when He yields; He rules after being enslaved; He lives after He has died; He completes His work after He Himself has been apparently cut off. His glory streams upon the dark ground of the deepest humiliation.[11]

We can only add that, apart from the Lord Jesus Christ, it would be impossible to understand this majestic chapter in Isaiah; and it would forever be a dark mystery without solution. However, in the light of His life, it has become the brightest star of Hebrew prophecy, the star of hope and salvation for all men.

ENDNOTES

[1] S. R. Driver and A. D. Neubauer, *The Fifty-third Chapter of Isaiah According to the Jewish Interpreters,* trans. Driver and Neubauer, James Parker & Co., Oxford and London, 1877, Vol. 2 (translations), p. 203.

[2] Ibid., p. 399.

[3] *The Soncino Talmud,* Rabbi Dr. I. Epstein (ed.), The Soncino Press, London, 1938, "Sukkah," p. 246.

[4] *The Soncino Talmud,* Rabbi Dr. I. Epstein (ed.), The Soncino Press, London, 1935, "Baba Metzia," p. 6.

[5] Driver and Neubauer, pp. 99-100.

[6] Ibid., pp. 437-440.

[7] Ibid., p. 445.

[8] Ibid., p. 114.

[9] *The Soncino Talmud,* "Sukkah," p. 246.

[10] Modern Hebrew dictionaries and official documents still spell the name Jesus as "Yeshu" instead of the correct "Yeshua."

[11] Franz Delitzsch, *Biblical Commentary on the Prophecies of Isaiah,* trans. Rev. James Martin, Eerdmans, Grand Rapids, 1949, Vol. II, p. 341.

POSTSCRIPT

Ten years after he began his work on *The Prophet Isaiah,* Dr. Victor Buksbazen completed his 500-page commentary, calling it "this labor of love."

In a beautifully written postscript, he praised God for His mercy and thanked his wife, Lydia, for her constant encouragement.

"When I started the work on Isaiah," he wrote, "I had only a general and vague idea of the magnitude of the task to which I had set my hand. But as one progressed, the enormity of the undertaking loomed ever larger before my eyes. Increasingly one became aware of his own inadequacy. Had I known from the beginning what I learned later, I might not have dared to start out. Nevertheless, the Spirit of the Lord kept spurring me on and encouraging me to finish what I started out to do.

"The completion of this commentary coincides with my seventieth birthday and with my retirement from the active, almost lifelong ministry as General Secretary of The Friends of Israel.

"'To God be the glory, great things He has done!'"

Victor Buksbazen
Collingswood, New Jersey, 1973

One year later, on October 23, 1974, the day after his seventy-first birthday, God called Dr. Buksbazen home peacefully. His ambassadorship to the lost sheep of the house of Israel and the world was completed. For more than thirty years he edited *Israel My Glory* magazine and dynamically led The Friends of Israel Gospel Ministry, Inc. His profound dedication to the work of Christ is still being felt today, and the legacies of his life and writings will continue to enrich all those who are privileged to come to know them.

DR. VICTOR BUKSBAZEN

VII.

THE PERSONAL TESTIMONY OF DR. VICTOR BUKSBAZEN (1903–1974)

"SURELY GOODNESS AND MERCY WILL FOLLOW ME ALL THE DAYS OF MY LIFE"

The above quotation from Psalm 23 describes perfectly the experiences of God's loving guidance in my life.

I was born in Warsaw, Poland, in the year 1903. My father, who was a box manufacturer, was at heart a devout seeker after the truth. His was a kind, loving, and gentle nature; and it was he who sought to instill into my young heart the knowledge and love of God. Even before I was born, my father, urged by a living quest after salvation, contacted some Jewish missionaries in Warsaw. At first he attended their meetings to repudiate the preaching of Christ as inconsistent with the teachings of Judaism. But God, through His blessed Word, spoke to his heart; and he believed on the Lord Jesus Christ.

When I was still a child of tender age, he took me to the mission so that my ear should become accustomed to the gospel sound; and on our way home he would explain to me, in terms intelligible to a little boy, the message that we had heard. I praise God for every remembrance of my father, for the blessed influence he had upon my life. It was he who also was my first teacher in reading; and, characteristically enough, he chose the Hebrew Bible as my textbook. Thus I literally was raised upon the Word of God and learned to love it ever since I can remember.

When the First World War Came

My childhood paradise, consisting of happy fellowship with my beloved parents and younger brother and sisters, seemed to collapse suddenly. Father was a sergeant in the

Russian army, and one early summer morning, he awoke me and told me he was leaving for the army.

He came back before the war was over, but broken in health. The Germans entered Warsaw and the surrounding provinces, and we moved into the country to escape starvation. However, hunger, misery, and disease followed us. Men were dying all around us either from hunger, epidemics, or cold.

When our family was living in a little Polish village and was in dire need of food and warm clothing, my father somehow secured from a farmer two large loaves of coarse rye bread, some of which he left with his family, and the remainder—about 40 pounds—he carried about 70 miles on his back to Warsaw, intending to sell it and buy warm clothing for his family with the proceeds. But on his arrival in Warsaw, after a two-day hike, he found starving children swollen with hunger in the streets. He then cut the bread into chunks and distributed it among the ravenous children. Two days later he came home empty-handed but with a face strangely radiant—it reflected Christ.

THE PERSONAL TESTIMONY OF DR. BUKSBAZEN

Eventually, my younger brother died; and soon after, my father, exhausted and undernourished, succumbed to the typhoid epidemic. Before he passed away, he asked me to take care of my mother and two sisters; and then he pleaded with me to study the Word of God and, if I should come to believe in the Lord Jesus Christ, to confess Him openly. He was buried in the little village cemetery under a young pine tree. Using a sharp knife, I left an identifying mark on that tree, hoping one day to return and erect a tombstone. But when I returned years later, the mark on the tree was gone, and I could find no trace of where his remains were buried. Thus a noble man and a sincere servant of the Lord passed away unknown to men. Yet I know his name is written in the Book of Life.

After his death I did my utmost to carry out the first part of his request. I cared for and supported my mother and sisters for many years, even during this present war until Pearl Harbor, when I lost touch with my loved ones. If they are still alive today, they are in the hands of that archenemy of the Jewish people, Adolph Hitler.

The sole contact I have with them is in prayer. I entreat all our readers to join with me, not only for them but also for all those other unhappy Jewish brethren who suffer horrors beyond our imagination.

When we returned to Warsaw from the country, I immediately sought out the mission where I first heard the gospel message. There the Lord revealed to me that I was a lost sinner in need of forgiveness and salvation; and I embraced Christ, who gave His life for me and purchased my salvation through His shed blood.

On May 2, 1922, I confessed Jesus Christ as my personal Savior in baptism. It is now more than 20 years since I gave my heart to Him; and I praise the Lord for these years of rich experience and sacred fellowship. My relatives, however, were very much against me at the time and sought with pleadings and threats to dissuade me from bringing on the family this "terrible disgrace." But the Lord enabled me to stand steadfast. Born and raised among the Jewish people and knowing them intimately, I realized their terrible distress. I know their frustration and disappointment; but I also know our

Messiah Jesus, who is able to fulfill all Israel's hopes and longings and save to the uttermost.

(Originally printed in *Israel My Glory* magazine, March 1943)